For Patty

Willow & Shannon

best wishes

Robert Aum

SUN UNDER WOOD

By Robert Hass

POETRY

Sun Under Wood
Human Wishes
Praise
Field Guide

ESSAYS

Twentieth Century Pleasures

TRANSLATIONS

Czeslaw Milosz, The Separate Notebooks (with Robert Pinsky and
    Renata Gorczynski)
Czeslaw Milosz, Unattainable Earth (with the author)
Czeslaw Milosz, Collected Poems (with the author and others)
Czeslaw Milosz, Provinces (with the author)
Czeslaw Milosz, Facing the River (with the author)
The Essential Haiku: Versions of Bashō, Buson, and Issa

EDITOR

Robinson Jeffers, Rock and Hawk: Shorter Poems
Tomas Tranströmer, Selected Poems: 1954–1986
Into the Garden: A Wedding Anthology (with Stephen Mitchell)

SUN
UNDER
WOOD

New Poems By

ROBERT HASS

THE ECCO PRESS

THE ECCO PRESS
100 West Broad Street
Hopewell, New Jersey 08525
Published simultaneously in Canada by
Penguin Books Canada Ltd., Ontario
Printed in the United States of America

Grateful acknowledgment to the following journals: *Agni Review, Antaeus, Colorado Review, Harvard Review, Michigan Quarterly Review, Threepenny Review, Triquarterly,* and *Zzyzyva.* "Sonnet" first appeared in *The New Yorker.*

Library of Congress Cataloging-in-Publication Data
Hass, Robert
Sun under wood : new poems / Robert Hass. — 1st ed.
     p.   cm.
ISBN 0-88001-468-7
I. Title
PS3558.A725S86   1996
811'.54 — dc20   96-19322

Designed by Jonathan Greene
The text of this book is set in Cochin.

9   8   7   6   5   4   3   2   1

FIRST EDITION

for Brenda

Now goth sonne under wode —
Me reweth, Marie, thi faire rode.
Now goth sonne under tre —
Me reweth, Marie, thi sonne and thee.
—Anonymous, 12th century

CONTENTS

SUN UNDER WOOD

HAPPINESS

Because yesterday morning from the steamy window
we saw a pair of red foxes across the creek
eating the last windfall apples in the rain—
they looked up at us with their green eyes
long enough to symbolize the wakefulness of living things
and then went back to eating—

and because this morning
when she went into the gazebo with her black pen and yellow pad
to coax an inquisitive soul
from what she thinks of as the reluctance of matter,
I drove into town to drink tea in the cafe
and write notes in a journal—mist rose from the bay
like the luminous and indefinite aspect of intention,
and a small flock of tundra swans
for the second winter in a row was feeding on new grass
in the soaked fields; they symbolize mystery, I suppose,
they are also called whistling swans, are very white,
and their eyes are black—

and because the tea steamed in front of me,
and the notebook, turned to a new page,
was blank except for a faint blue idea of order,

I wrote: *happiness! it is December, very cold,*
we woke early this morning,
and lay in bed kissing,
our eyes squinched up like bats.

OUR LADY OF THE SNOWS

In white,
the unpainted statue of the young girl
on the side altar
made the quality of mercy seem scrupulous and calm.

When my mother was in a hospital drying out,
or drinking at a pace that would put her there soon,
I would slip in the side door,
light an aromatic candle,
and bargain for us both.
Or else I'd stare into the day-moon of that face
and, if I concentrated, fly.

Come down! come down!
she'd call, because I was so high.

Though mostly when I think of myself
at that age, I am standing at my older brother's closet
studying the shirts,
convinced that I could be absolutely transformed
by something I could borrow.
And the days churned by,
navigable sorrow.

DRAGONFLIES MATING

1.

The people who lived here before us
also loved these high mountain meadows on summer mornings.
They made their way up here in easy stages
when heat began to dry the valleys out,
following the berry harvest probably and the pine buds:
climbing and making camp and gathering,
then breaking camp and climbing and making camp and gathering.
A few miles a day. They sent out the children
to dig up bulbs of the mariposa lilies that they liked to roast
at night by the fire where they sat talking about how this year
was different from last year. Told stories,
knew where they were on earth from the names,
owl moon, bear moon, gooseberry moon.

2.

Jaime de Angulo (1934) was talking to a Channel Island Indian
in a Santa Barbara bar. You tell me how your people said
the world was made. Well, the guy said, Coyote was on the
  mountain

and he had to pee. Wait a minute, Jaime said,
I was talking to a Pomo the other day and he said
Red Fox made the world. They say Red Fox, the guy shrugged,
we say Coyote. So, he had to pee
and he didn't want to drown anybody, so he turned toward the
    place
where the ocean would be. Wait a minute, Jaime said,
if there were no people yet, how could he drown anybody?
The Channelleño got a funny look on his face. You know,
he said, when I was a kid, I wondered about that,
and I asked my father. We were living up toward Santa Ynez.
He was sitting on a bench in the yard shaving down fence posts
with an ax, and I said, how come Coyote was worried about
    people
when he had to pee and there were no people? The guy laughed.
And my old man looked up at me with this funny smile
and said, You know, when I was a kid, I wondered about that.

3.

Thinking about that story just now, early morning heat,
first day in the mountains, I remembered stories about sick Indians
and—in the same thought—standing on the free throw line.

St. Raphael's parish, where the northern-most of the missions
had been, was founded as a hospital, was named for the angel
in the scriptures who healed the blind man with a fish

he laid across his eyes. — I wouldn't mind being that age again,
hearing those stories, eyes turned upward toward the young nun
in her white, fresh-smelling, immaculately laundered robes. —

The Franciscan priests who brought their faith in God
across the Atlantic, brought with the baroque statues and
   metalwork crosses
and elaborately embroidered cloaks, influenza and syphilis and the
   coughing disease.

Which is why we settled an almost empty California.
There were drawings in the mission museum of the long, dark
   wards
full of small brown people, wasted, coughing into blankets,

the saintly Franciscan fathers moving patiently among them.
It would, Sister Marietta said, have broken your hearts to see it.
They meant so well, she said, and such a terrible thing

came here with their love. And I remembered how I hated it
after school — because I loved basketball practice more than
   anything
on earth — that I never knew if my mother was going to show up

well into one of those weeks of drinking she disappeared into,
and humiliate me in front of my classmates with her bright,
   confident eyes,

and slurred, though carefully pronounced words, and the
   appalling

impromptu sets of mismatched clothes she was given to
when she had the dim idea of making a good impression in that
   state.
Sometimes from the gym floor with its sweet, heady smell of
   varnish

I'd see her in the entryway looking for me, and I'd bounce
the ball two or three times, study the orange rim as if it were,
which it was, the true level of the world, the one sure thing

the power in my hands could summon. I'd bounce the ball
once more, feel the grain of the leather in my fingertips and shoot.
It was a perfect thing; it was almost like killing her.

   4.

When we say "mother" in poems,
we usually mean some woman in her late twenties
or early thirties trying to raise a child.

We use this particular noun
to secure the pathos of the child's point of view
and to hold her responsible.

5.

If you're afraid now?
Fear is a teacher.
Sometimes you thought that
Nothing could reach her,
Nothing can reach you.
Wouldn't you rather
Sit by the river, sit
On the dead bank,
Deader than winter,
Where all the roots gape?

6.

This morning in the early sun,
steam rising from the pond the color of smoky topaz,
a pair of delicate, copper-red, needle-fine insects
are mating in the unopened crown of a Shasta daisy
just outside your door. The green flowerheads look like wombs
or the upright, supplicant bulbs of a vegetal pre-erection.
The insect lovers seem to be transferring the cosmos into each
    other
by attaching at the tail, holding utterly still, and quivering intently.

I think (on what evidence?) that they are different from us.
That they mate and are done with mating.

They don't carry all this half-mated longing up out of childhood
and then go looking for it everywhere.
And so, I think, they can't wound each other the way we do.
They don't go through life dizzy or groggy with their hunger,
kill with it, smear it on everything, though it is perhaps also true
that nothing happens to them quite like what happens to us
when the blue-backed swallow dips swiftly toward the green pond
and the pond's green-and-blue reflected swallow marries it a
    moment
in the reflected sky and the heart goes out to the end of the rope
it has been throwing into abyss after abyss, and a singing
    shimmers
from every color the morning has risen into.

My insect instructors have stilled, they are probably stuck
    together
in some bliss and minute pulse of after-longing
evolution worked out to suck the last juice of the world
into the receiver body. They can't separate probably
until it is done.

MY MOTHER'S NIPPLES

They're where all displacement begins.
They bulldozed the upper meadow at Squaw Valley,
where horses from the stable, two chestnuts, one white,
grazed in the mist and the scent of wet grass on summer mornings
and moonrise threw the owl's shadow on voles and wood rats
crouched in the sage smell the earth gave back after dark
with the day's heat to the night air.
And after the framers began to pound nails
and the electricians and plumbers came around to talk specs
with the general contractor, someone put up the green sign
with alpine daisies on it that said Squaw Valley Meadows.
They had gouged up the deep-rooted bunchgrass
and the wet alkali-scented earth had been pushed aside
or trucked someplace out of the way, and they poured concrete
and laid road—pleasant scent of tar in the spring sun—

—◆—

"He wanted to get out of his head," she said,
"so I told him to write about his mother's nipples."

—◆—

The cosmopolitan's song on this subject:

[12]

Alors! les nipples de ma mère!

The romantic's song

What could be more fair
than les nipples de ma mère?

The utopian's song

I will freely share
les nipples de ma mère.

The philosopher's song

Here was always there
with les nipples de ma mère

The capitalist's song

Fifty cents a share

The saint's song

Lift your eyes in prayer

The misanthrope's song

I can scarcely bear

The melancholic's song

They were never there,
les nipples de ma mère.
They are not anywhere.

The indigenist's song

And so the boy they called Loves His Mother's Tits
Went into the mountains and fasted for three days.
On the fourth he saw a red-tailed hawk with broken wings,
On the fifth a gored doe in a ravine, entrails
Spilled onto the rocks, eye looking up at him
From the twisted neck. All the sixth day he was dizzy
And his stomach hurt. On the seventh he made three deep cuts
In the meat of his palm. He entered the pain at noon
And an eagle came to him crying three times like the mewling
A doe makes planting her hooves in the soft duff for mating
And he went home and they called him Eagle Three Times after
    that.

The regionalist's song

Los Pechos.
Rolling oak woodland between Sierra pines
and the simmering valley.

Pink, of course, soft; a girl's—
She wore white muslin tennis outfits
in the style Helen Wills made fashionable.
Trim athletic swimsuits.
A small person, compact body. In the photographs
she's on the beach, standing straight,
hands on hips, grinning,
eyes desperate even then.

Mothers in the nineteen forties didn't nurse.
I never saw her naked. Oh! yes, I did,
once, but I can't remember. I remember
not wanting to.

Two memories. My mother had been drinking for several days, and
I had thought dinner would be cancelled, so I wouldn't get to watch
The Lone Ranger on my aunt's and uncle's television set. But we went
to dinner and my aunt with her high-pitched voice took the high-
minded tone that she took in my mother's presence. She had put out
hard candies in little cut glass dishes as she always did, and we ate
dinner, at which water was served to the grown-ups, and no one
spoke except my uncle who teased us in his English accent. A tall
man. He used to pat me on the head too hard and say, "Robert of
Sicily, brother of the Pope Urbane." And after dinner when the tele-

vision was turned on in the immaculate living room and Silver was running across the snowy screen, his mane shuddering from the speed, the door bell rang. It was two men in white coats and my mother bolted from the table into the kitchen and out the back door. The men went in after her. The back stairs led into a sort of well between the houses, and when I went into the kitchen I could hear her screaming, "No! no!," the sound echoing and re-echoing among the houses.

Some years later. I am perhaps ten, eleven. We are visiting my mother on the parklike grounds of the State Hospital in the Napa Valley. It is Sunday again. Green lawns, the heavy sweet scent of mock orange. Many of the patients are walking, alone or with their families, on the paths. One man seemed to be giving speeches to a tree. I had asked my grandmother why, if my mother had a drinking problem, that's the phrase I had been taught to use, why she was locked up with crazy people. It was a question I could have asked my father, but I understood that his answer would not be dependable. My grandmother said, with force, she had small red curls on her forehead, dressed with great style, you had better ask your father that. Then she thought better of it, and said, They have a treatment program, dear, maybe it will help. I tried out that phrase, treatment program. My mother was sitting on a bench. She looked immensely sad, seemed to have shrunk. Her hair was pulled across her forehead and secured with a white beret, like Teresa Wright in the movies. At first my brother and I just sat next to her on the bench and cried. My father held my sister's hand. My grandmother and grandfather stood to one side, a separate group, and watched.

Later, while they talked, I studied a middle-aged woman sitting on the next bench talking to herself in a foreign language. She was wearing a floral print dress and she spoke almost in a whisper but with passion, looking around from time to time, quick little furtive resentful glances. She was so careless of herself that I could see her breast, the brown nipple, when she leaned forward. I didn't want to look, and looked, and looked away.

⤙⤚

Hot Sierra morning.
Brenda working in another room.
Rumble of heavy equipment in the meadow,
bird squall, Steller's jay, and then
the piercing three-note whistle of a robin.
They're mating now. Otherwise they're mute.
Mother-ing. Or Mother-song.
Mother-song-song-song.

⤙⤚

We used to laugh, my brother and I in college,
about the chocolate cake. Tears in our eyes laughing.
In grammar school, whenever she'd start to drink,
she panicked and made amends by baking chocolate cake.
And, of course, when we got home, we'd smell the strong, sweet
    smell
of the absolute darkness of chocolate,
and be too sick to eat it.

⤙⤚

The first girl's breasts I saw
were the Chevy dealer's daughter Linda Wren's.
Pale in the moonlight. Little nubbins, pink-nosed.
I can still hear the slow sound of the surf
of my breath drawing in. I think I almost fainted.

⊰⊱

Twin fonts of mercy, they used to say of the Virgin's breasts
in the old liturgy the Irish priests
could never quite handle, it being a form of bodily reference,
springs of grace, freshets
of lovingkindness. If I remember correctly,
there are baroque poems in this spirit
in which each of Christ's wounds is a nipple.
Drink and live: this is the son's blood.

⊰⊱

Dried figs, candied roses.

What is one to say of the nipples of old women
who would, after all, find the subject
unseemly.

Yesterday I ran along the edge of the meadow in the heat
of late afternoon. So many wildflowers
tangled in the grass. So many grasses—
reedgrass, the bentgrass and timothy, little quaking grass,

dogtail, rip-gut brome—the seeds flaring from the stalks
in tight chevrons of green and purple-green
but loosening.

I said to myself:
some things do not blossom in this life.

I said: what we've lost is a story
and what we've never had
a song.

When my father died, I was curious to see in what ratio she would feel relieved and lost. All during the days of his dying, she stood by his bed talking to whichever of her children was present about the food in the cafeteria or the native state of the nurses—"She's from Portland, isn't that interesting? Your Aunt Nell lived in Portland when Owen was working for the Fisheries."—and turn occasionally to my father who was half-conscious, his eyes a morphine cloud, and say, in a sort of baby talk, "It's all right, dear. It's all right." And after he died, she was dazed, and clearly did not know herself whether she felt relieved or lost, and I felt sorry for her that she had no habit and so no means of self-knowing. She was waiting for us to leave so she could start drinking. Only once was she suddenly alert. When the young man from the undertaker's came and explained that she would need a copy of her marriage license in order to do something about the insurance and pensions, she looked briefly alive, anxious, and I realized that, though she rarely told the truth, she was a very poor dissembler. Now her eyes were a young girl's. What, she asked, if someone just couldn't turn up a marriage license; it seemed such a detail, there must be cases. I could see that she was trying out avenues of escape, and I was thinking, now what? They were never married? I told her not to worry. I'd locate it. She considered this and said it would be fine. I could see she had made some decision, and then she grew indefinite again.

So, back in California, it was with some interest that I retraced the drive from San Francisco to Santa Rosa which my parents made in 1939, when according to my mother's story — it was the first account of it I'd ever heard — she and my father had eloped. The Sonoma County Office of Records was in a pink cinder-block building landscaped with reptilian pink oleanders which were still blooming in the Indian summer heat. It would have been raining when my parents drove that road in an old (I imagined) cream-colored Packard convertible I had seen one photo of. I asked the woman at the desk for the marriage certificate for February 1939. I wondered what the surprise was going to be, and it was a small one. No problem, Mrs. Minh said. But you had the date wrong, so it took me a while to find it. It was October, not February. Driving back to San Francisco, I had time to review this information. My brother was born in December 1939. Hard to see that it meant anything except that my father had tried very hard to avoid his fate. I felt so sorry for them. That they thought it was worth keeping a secret. Or, more likely, that their life together began in a negotiation too painful to be referred to again. That my mother had, with a certain fatality, let me pick up the license, so her first son would not know the circumstance of his conception. I felt sorry for her shame, for my father's panic. It finished off my dim wish that there had been an early romantic or ecstatic time in their lives, a blossoming, brief as a northern summer maybe, but a blossoming.

What we've never had is a song
and what we've really had is a song.
Sweet smell of timothy in the meadow.
Clouds massing east above the ridge in a sky
as blue as the mountain lakes,
so there are places on this earth clear all the way up
and all the way down
and in between a various blossoming,
the many seed shapes of the many things
finding their way into flower or not,
that the wind scatters.

There are all kinds of emptiness and fullness
that sing and do not sing.

I said: you are her singing.

I came home from school and she was gone. I don't know what in-stinct sent me to the park. I suppose it was the only place I could think of where someone might hide: she had passed out under an or-ange tree, curled up. Her face, flushed, eyelids swollen, was a ruin. Though I needed urgently to know whatever was in it, I could hardly bear to look. When I couldn't wake her, I decided to sit with her until she woke up. I must have been ten years old: I suppose I

wanted for us to look like a son and mother who had been picnick-
ing, like a mother who had fallen asleep in the warm light and scent
of orange blossoms and a boy who was sitting beside her daydream-
ing, not thinking about anything in particular.

You are not her singing, though she is what's
broken in a song.
She is its silences.

She may be its silences.

Hawk drifting in the blue air,
grey of the granite ridges,
incense cedars, pines.

I tried to think of some place on earth she loved.

I remember she only ever spoke happily
of high school.

THE GARDENS OF WARSAW

The rain loves the afternoon and the tall lime trees
just where the broad Avenue of the Third of May
crosses Jerozolimska Street (it is 1922)
have carved green channels deep into the summer.
Above the dusty pavements, darkening only faintly
when the clouds pass over, above clanging trolleys
and the glistening Vistula flinging the broken forms
of trees and clouds and bridges back into the sky,
above the Virgin's statue on the Street of Honey Cakes,
above the Church of the Holy Cross where Chopin's heart,
in a glimmering silver box, is turning to fine dust,
above the kiosks with their posters of Clara Bow and Chaplin
and Valentino as The Sheik, above the crowded tenements
huddled around courtyards, above new apartment houses
with mansard roofs, Viennese grilles, King Tut carvings,
sylph-like women frosted into glass, it is raining a light rain.
It rains on the Saxon Gardens, lilacs and apple trees
on the grassy slopes, and on the Ujazdowski Gardens
with their chain of ponds where the black-billed swans
paddle calmly under the archways of miniature bridges
and a Zionist boy is reading a book on a wooden bench.
It rains on the Botanical Gardens where the magnolias,
blooming, toss off grails of pure white idly.

It rains also on the Lazieniki Gardens lightly
and the small palace with its cream-colored walls
and columned porticoes shimmering in the bull's-eye
circles-within-circles the rain makes lightly
on the face of the lagoon and on the feathers of nightingales
furtive in the elms and on the bronze statue of Stanislaus
in the sweet scent of the orangery where water laps
against the mottled marble stairs of the amphitheater
where Paderewski once conducted Brahms, and even the children,
chasing each other on the grass across the way,
or turning in fast circles, arms out, till they fall down
into their dizziness, stopped at a sudden yearning lift
of the violins, and listened. It is summer as I write,
Northern California. Clear air, a blazing sky in August,
bright shy Audubon's warblers in the pines.
I have been reading an old travel guide I found,
bound in dark blue cloth with gilded scrollwork titles,
in a used bookstore in this little mountain town.
It is inscribed, "From Cazimir to Hilda,
with patient hope and deep respect. Come back,
my dear. Be sure to see the bell of Krakow."
The children clear the table, fetch fleecy towels
for the beach. Congress in recess, guards sleeping
at the embassies. Even the murderers are on vacation.

LAYOVER

Thin snow falling on the runway at Anchorage,
bundled bodies of men, grey padded jackets, outsized gloves,
heads bent against the wind. They lunge, weaving
among the scattering of luggage carts, hard at what must be
half the world's work, loading and unloading.

Mounded snow faintly grey and sculpted into what seems
the entire vocabulary of resignation. It shines
in the one patch of sun, is lustered with the precipitate
of the exhaust of turbine engines, the burnt carbons
of pre-Cambrian forests, life feeding life
feeding life in the usual, mindless way. The colonizer's
usual prefab, low-roofed storage sheds in the distance
pale beige and curiously hopeful in their upright verticals
like boys in an army, or like the spruce and hemlock forest
on low hillsides beyond them. And beyond those, half seen
in the haze, range after range of snowy mountains
in the valleys of which—moose feeding along the frozen streams,
snow foxes hunting ptarmigan in the brilliant whiteness—
no human could survive for very long, and which it is the
    imagination's
intensest, least possible longing to inhabit.

This is a day of diplomatic lull. Iraq seems to have agreed
to withdraw from Kuwait with Russian assurances
that the government of Hussein will be protected. It won't happen,
thousands of young men will be killed, shot, blown up,
buried in the sand, an ancient city bombed,
but one speaks this way of countries, as if they were entities
with wills. Iraq has agreed. Russia has promised. A bleak thing,

dry snow melting on the grizzled, salted tarmac.
One of the men on the airstrip is waving his black,
monstrously gloved hands at someone. Almost dancing:
strong body, rhythmic, efficient stride. He knows
what he's supposed to do. He's getting our clothes to us
at the next stop. Flowerburst ties, silky underwear.
There are three young Indians, thin faces, high cheekbones,
skin the color of old brass, chatting quietly across from me
in what must be an Athabascan dialect. A small child crying
mildly, sleepily, down the way, a mother murmuring in English.
Soft hum of motors stirring through the plane's low, dim fuselage
the stale air, breathed and breathed, we have been sharing.

NOTES ON "LAYOVER"

I could have said that I am a listless eye gazing through watery glass on a Friday afternoon in February. A raven flies by. If he cries out sharply, I can't hear him. Strong wingbeats. Very black against grey sky, white snow.

I could have said that Alaska—*where the sea breaks its back*, in one of the languages of the people who looked for centuries at water lashing and lashing against jagged rock, mists of spray blown toward them by Aleutian winds—still feels like a military colony, which is the way a wilderness is settled, and is, ultimately, why I happen to be here.

And that the woman with the baby is the wife of some technician whose rank she knows well from filling out forms to do with the delivery of her child and an ovarian cyst she had removed and discount airfares for the relatives of ALASCOM personnel, and also because it is a form of hope, grade seven, soon to be grade six.

And that, watching the men unload the luggage, I was thinking of her body, and then of her underwear. Pretty, not very expensive, neatly folded for the journey.

A way of locating itself that even the idle mind works at. Airports:

people dressed well and not well, hope and exhaustion, reunions, separations. Families with banners and flowers, WELCOME HOME SUSIE, and the beaming unsexual smiles of family loyalty, and floral sprays in cellophane. Men with clean shirts in rayon bags smoking in the limbo between sales presentations—"I just admit flat out" overheard on the flight in "that we've had a little problem with distribution and that the home office knows it has to get its act together, so we're pricing real competitively, and if they place an order right now" words that can stare down any hopelessness "they got a good chance of getting theirselves a hell of a deal." Nursing slim glasses of beer in the lounges—each sip stranding a little line of foam—to the sound of daytime talk shows on men who sleep with their mothers-in-law, transvestites, filmed three thousand miles away, transmitted to the heavens and bounced back in little waves and dots and flurries of ionized air carrying the peculiar contents of human curiosity. The sweet bleating of the baby, part whimper, part croon now, to take its place in this vast, deeply strange net of contingencies. An old poem by an old poet composed on islands to the southwest of here; he must have been on a fishing boat: The whitebait/opens its black eye/in the net of the law.

I could have said a translation of the Athabascan idiom for "good-bye" is "make prayers to the raven." Anyone who has walked in a northern forest knows what sense it makes. Sharp echoing cry in the pine wood and the snow. Swift black flash of its flight, and the powerful wings. Ruthless and playful spirit of creation. World's truth in the black bead of its eye.

That all crossings over are a way of knowing, and of knowing we don't know, where we have been: a man leaves one woman for another and wakes up in a room with morning light and a vase he doesn't recognize, full of hydrangeas, mauve petals of hydrangeas.

THE WOODS IN NEW JERSEY

Where there was only grey, and brownish grey,
And greyish brown against the white
Of fallen snow at twilight in the winter woods,

Now an uncanny flamelike thing, black
and sulphur-yellow, as if it were dreamed by Audubon,
Is turned upside down in a delicate cascade

Of new green leaves, feeding on whatever mites
Or small white spiders haunt underleafs at stem end.
A magnolia warbler, to give the thing a name.

The other name we give this overmuch of appetite
And beauty unconscious of itself is life.
And that that kept the mind becalmed all winter? —

The more austere and abstract rhythm of the trunks,
Vertical music the cold makes visible,
That holds the whole thing up and gives it form,

or strength — call that the law. It's made,
whatever we like to think, more of interests
than of reasons, trees reaching each their own way

for the light, to make the sort of order that there is.
And what of those deer threading through the woods
In a late snowfall and silent as the snow?

Look: they move among the winter trees, so much
the color of the trees, they hardly seem to move.

for Justice William J. Brennan, Jr

IOWA CITY: EARLY APRIL

This morning a cat—bright orange—pawing at the one patch of
   new grass in the sand- and tanbark-colored leaves.

And last night the sapphire of the raccoon's eyes in the beam of the
   flashlight.
He was climbing a tree beside the house, trying to get onto the
   porch, I think, for a wad of oatmeal
Simmered in cider from the bottom of the pan we'd left out for the
   birds.

And earlier a burnished, somewhat dazed woodchuck, his coat
   gleaming with spring,
Loping toward his burrow in the roots of a tree among the drying
   winter's litter
Of old leaves on the floor of the woods, when I went out to get the
   New York Times.

And male cardinals whistling back and forth—sireeep, sreeep,
   sreeep—
Sets of three sweet full notes, weaving into and out of each other
   like the triplet rhymes in medieval poetry,
And the higher, purer notes of the tufted titmice among them,

High in the trees where they were catching what they could of the
  early sun.

And a doe and two yearlings, picking their way along the worrying
  path they'd made through the gully, their coats the color of the
  forest floor,
Stopped just at the roots of the great chestnut where the
  woodchuck's burrow was,
Froze, and the doe looked back over her shoulder at me for a long
  moment, and leapt forward,
Her young following, and bounded with that almost mincing
  precision in the landing of each hoof
Up the gully, over it, and out of sight. So that I remembered
Dreaming last night that a deer walked into the house while I was
  writing at the kitchen table,
Came in the glass door from the garden, looked at me with a stilled
  defiant terror, like a thing with no choices,
And, neck bobbing in that fragile-seeming, almost mechanical mix
  of arrest and liquid motion, came to the table
And snatched a slice of apple, and stood, and then quietened, and
  to my surprise did not leave again.

And those little captains, the chickadees, swift to the feeder and
  swift away.

And the squirrels with their smoke-plume tails trailing digging in
  the leaves to bury or find buried—

I'm told they don't remember where they put things, that it's an
    activity of incessant discovery—
Nuts, tree-fall proteins, whatever they forage from around the
    house of our leavings,

And the flameheaded woodpecker at the suet with his black-and-
    white ladderback elegant fierceness—
They take sunflower seeds and stash them in the rough ridges of
    the tree's bark
Where the beaks of the smoke-and-steel blue nuthatches can't
    quite get at them—
Though the nuthatches sometimes seem to get them as they con
    the trees methodically for spiders' eggs or some other
    overwintering insect's intricately packaged lump of futurity
Got from its body before the cold came on.

And the little bat in the kitchen lightwell—
When I climbed on a chair to remove the sheet of wimpled plastic
    and let it loose,
It flew straight into my face and I toppled to the floor, chair under
    me,
And it flared down the hall and did what seemed a frantic
    reconnoiter of the windowed, high-walled living room.
And lit on a brass firelog where it looked like a brown and ash
    grey teenaged suede glove with Mephistophelean dreams,
And then, spurt of black sperm, up, out the window, and into the
    twilight woods.

All this life going on about my life, or living a life about all this life
 going on,
Being a creature, whatever my drama of the moment, at the edge
 of the raccoon's world —
He froze in my flashlight beam and looked down, no affect, just
 looked,
The ringtail curled and flared to make him look bigger and not to
 be messed with —
I was thinking he couldn't know how charming his comic-book
 robber's mask was to me,
That his experience of his being and mine of his and his of mine
 were things entirely apart,
Though there were between us, probably, energies of shrewd and
 respectful tact, based on curiosity and fear —
I knew about his talons whatever he knew about me —
And as for my experience of myself, it comes and goes, I'm not
 sure it's any one thing, as my experience of these creatures is
 not,
And I know I am often too far from it or too near, glad to be rid of
 it which is why it was such a happiness,
The bright orange of the cat, and the first pool of green grass-
 leaves in early April, and the birdsong — that orange and that
 green not colors you'd set next to one another in the human
 scheme.

And the crows' calls, even before you open your eyes, at sunup.

A NOTE ON "IOWA CITY:
EARLY APRIL"

The raccoon stared down from the crotch of a tree.
A dark night, icy in the early spring.

"This naturalist I admire," I said, "says that every species
lives in its own sensory world."

The raccoon stared down; he was silent.

"He also said that we may come to know enough about the human
    brain to diagnose and correct for the deformations
imposed by evolution on the human senses
    and arrive at something like objective truth."

The raccoon was silent.

"Maybe," I volunteered, "they can do something about raccoon
deformation."

He might have been thinking "deformed from what?"
    but I don't think so; he was silent.

He might have been trying to discern
    under the odor of garlic and rosemary on my fingers,

and under the smell of oatmeal soap under that,
    the smell of sex from a sweet hour when we lay down and the
    snow fell in quick flurries
in the early afternoon; he may have been smelling toward
    some distant cousin to the smell that is pistil and stamen
from which flowers the raccoon-universe.

Maybe that, but I don't know. The raccoon was silent.

He might have been studying an enemy,
   he might simply have been curious,
but I don't know.

So I entered the silence, and was glad to be in it for a while,
    knowing I couldn't stay.
It smelled like snow and pine and the winter dark,
    though it was my silence, not his,
        and there was nothing there.

for E. O. Wilson

SONNET

A man talking to his ex-wife on the phone.
He has loved her voice and listens with attention
to every modulation of its tone. Knowing
it intimately. Not knowing what he wants
from the sound of it, from the tendered civility.
He studies, out the window, the seed shapes
of the broken pods of ornamental trees.
The kind that grow in everyone's garden, that no one
but horticulturists can name. Four arched chambers
of pale green, tiny vegetal proscenium arches,
a pair of black tapering seeds bedded in each chamber.
A wish geometry, miniature, Indian or Persian,
lovers or gods in their apartments. Outside, white,
patient animals, and tangled vines, and rain.

FAINT MUSIC

Maybe you need to write a poem about grace.

When everything broken is broken,
and everything dead is dead,
and the hero has looked into the mirror with complete contempt,
and the heroine has studied her face and its defects
remorselessly, and the pain they thought might,
as a token of their earnestness, release them from themselves
has lost its novelty and not released them,
and they have begun to think, kindly and distantly,
watching the others go about their days —
likes and dislikes, reasons, habits, fears —
that self-love is the one weedy stalk
of every human blossoming, and understood,
therefore, why they had been, all their lives,
in such a fury to defend it, and that no one —
except some almost inconceivable saint in his pool
of poverty and silence — can escape this violent, automatic
life's companion ever, maybe then, ordinary light,
faint music under things, a hovering like grace appears.

As in the story a friend told once about the time
he tried to kill himself. His girl had left him.

Bees in the heart, then scorpions, maggots, and then ash.
He climbed onto the jumping girder of the bridge,
the bay side, a blue, lucid afternoon.
And in the salt air he thought about the word "seafood,"
that there was something faintly ridiculous about it.
No one said "landfood." He thought it was degrading to the
    rainbow perch
he'd reeled in gleaming from the cliffs, the black rockbass,
scales like polished carbon, in beds of kelp
along the coast—and he realized that the reason for the word
was crabs, or mussels, clams. Otherwise
the restaurants could just put "fish" up on their signs,
and when he woke—he'd slept for hours, curled up
on the girder like a child—the sun was going down
and he felt a little better, and afraid. He put on the jacket
he'd used for a pillow, climbed over the railing
carefully, and drove home to an empty house.

There was a pair of her lemon yellow panties
hanging on a doorknob. He studied them. Much-washed.
A faint russet in the crotch that made him sick
with rage and grief. He knew more or less
where she was. A flat somewhere on Russian Hill.
They'd have just finished making love. She'd have tears
in her eyes and touch his jawbone gratefully. "God,"
she'd say, "you are so good for me." Winking lights,
a foggy view downhill toward the harbor and the bay.
"You're sad," he'd say. "Yes." "Thinking about Nick?"

"Yes," she'd say and cry. "I tried so hard," sobbing now,
"I really tried so hard." And then he'd hold her for a while—
Guatemalan weavings from his fieldwork on the wall—
and then they'd fuck again, and she would cry some more,
and go to sleep.
              And he, he would play that scene
once only, once and a half, and tell himself
that he was going to carry it for a very long time
and that there was nothing he could do
but carry it. He went out onto the porch, and listened
to the forest in the summer dark, madrone bark
cracking and curling as the cold came up.

It's not the story though, not the friend
leaning toward you, saying "And then I realized—,"
which is the part of stories one never quite believes.
I had the idea that the world's so full of pain
it must sometimes make a kind of singing.
And that the sequence helps, as much as order helps—
First an ego, and then pain, and then the singing.

FORTY SOMETHING

She says to him, musing, "If you ever leave me,
and marry a younger woman and have another baby,
I'll put a knife in your heart." They are in bed,
so she climbs onto his chest, and looks directly
down into his eyes. "You understand? Your heart."

SHAME: AN ARIA

You think you've grown up in various ways
and then the elevator door opens and you're standing inside
reaming out your nose—something about the dry air
in the mountains—and find yourself facing two spruce elderly
    couples
dressed like improbable wildflowers in their primary color
definitely on vacation sports outfits, a wormy curl of one of the
    body's
shameful and congealed lubricants gleaming on your fingertip
under the fluorescent lights, and there really isn't too much to say
as you descend the remaining two flights with them in silence,
all five of you staring straight ahead in this commodious
aluminium group coffin toward the ground floor. You are,
of course, trying to think of something witty to say. Your hand
is, of course, in your pocket discreetly transferring the offending
    article
into its accumulation of lint. One man clears his throat
and you admit to yourself that there are kinds of people—if not
people in particular—you hate, that these are they,
and that your mind is nevertheless, is nevertheless working
like a demented cicada drying its wings after rain to find some way
to save yourself in your craven, small child's large ego's idea

of their eyes. You even crank it up a notch, getting more high-
    minded
and lugubrious in the seconds it takes for the almost silent
gears and oiled hydraulic or pneumatic plungers and cables
of the machine to set you down. "Nosepicking," you imagine
    explaining
to the upturned, reverential faces, "is in a way the ground floor
of being. The body's fluids and solids, its various despised disjecta,
toenail parings left absently on the bedside table that your lover
the next night notices there, shit streaks in underwear or little,
    faint,
odorous pee-blossoms of the palest polleny color, the stiffened
small droplets in the sheets of the body's shuddering late-night
    loneliness
and self-love, russets of menstrual blood, toejam, earwax,
phlegm, the little dead militias of white corpuscles
we call pus, what are they after all but the twins of the juices
of mortal glory: sap, wine, breast milk, sperm, and blood. The
    most intimate hygienes,
those deepest tribal rules that teach a child
trying to struggle up out of the fear of loss of love
from anger, hatred, fear, they get taught to us, don't they,
as boundaries, terrible thresholds, what can be said (or thought, or
    done)
inside the house but not out, what can be said (or thought, or
    done)
only by oneself, which must therefore best not be done at all,
so that the core of the self, we learn early, is where shame lives

and where we also learn doubleness, and a certain practical
    cunning,
and what a theater is, and the ability to lie—"
the elevator has opened and closed, the silver-haired columbines
of the mountain are murmuring over breakfast menus in a room
    full of bright plastics
somewhere, and you, grown up in various ways, are at the
    typewriter,
thinking of all the slimes and jellies of decay, thinking
that the zombie passages, ghoul corridors, radiant death's-head
entries to that realm of terror claim us in the sick, middle-of-the-
    night
sessions of self-hatred and remorse, in the day's most hidden,
watchful self, the man not farting in the line at the bank,
no trace of discomfort on his mild, neighbor-loving face, the
    woman
calculating the distance to the next person she can borrow a
    tampon from
while she smiles attentively into this new man's explanation
of his theory about deforestation, claims us also, by seepage, in our
    lies,
small malices, razor knicks on the skin of others of our
    meannesses,
deprivations, rage, and what to do but face that way
and praise the kingdom of the dead, praise the power which we
    have all kinds
of phrases to elide, that none of us can worm our way out of—
"which all must kneel to in the end," "that no man can evade,"

[45   ]

praise it by calling it time, say it is master of the seasons,

mistress of the moment of the hunting hawk's sudden sheen of
   grape-brown

gleaming in the morning sun, the characteristic slow gesture,

two fingers across the cheekbone deliberately, of the lover
   dreamily

oiling her skin, in this moment, no other, before she turns to you

the face she wants you to see and the rest

that she hopes, when she can't keep it hidden, you can somehow
   love

and which, if you could love yourself, you would.

REGALIA
FOR A BLACK HAT DANCER

In the morning, after running along the river:
'Creekstones practice the mild yoga of becoming smooth.'
By afternoon I was thinking: once you're smooth, you're dead.
'It is good sometimes that poetry should disenchant us,'
I wrote, and something about 'the heart's huge vacancy,'
which seemed contemptible. After dinner—sudden cooling
of the summer air—I sat down to it. Where.

≁

Walking down to Heart's Desire beach in the summer evenings
of the year my marriage ended—

though I was hollowed out by pain,
honeycombed with the emptiness of it,
like the bird bones on the beach
the salt of the bay water had worked on for a season—
such surprising lightness in the hand—
I don't think I could have told the pain of loss
from the pain of possibility,
though I knew they weren't the same thing.

When I think of that time, I think mainly of the osprey's cry,
a startled yelp,

the cry more a color than a sound, and as if
it ripped the sky, was white,
as if it were scar tissue and fresh hurt at once.

Toyon, old oak, and coffeeberry: always about halfway,
but especially if the day had been hot, the scent of vanilla grass —
my throat so swollen with some unsortable mix
of sorrow and desire I couldn't swallow —
salt smell, grey water, sometimes the fog came in,
pouring down the dragonback of pines,
often there was one blue heron in the tidal pond —

and I'd present my emptiness, which has huge, baffled
(Rilke writing in French because there was no German equivalent
for *l'absence* in 'the great positive sense'
with which it appeared in Valéry:
one of my minor occupations was raging against Rilke),
and most of the time I felt nothing,
when the moment came that was supposed to embody presence,
nothing really. There were a few buffleheads,
as usual, a few gulls rocking in the surf.
Sometimes a Western grebe diving and swimming
with its crazed red eye.

So there were these two emptiness: one made of pain and desire
and one made of vacancy.

(Paused for a moment in this writing and went out.
Dark, first the dark. Wind in the trees.
Everybody's private pain: in Korea once, in a mountain pass,
a carved placatory shrine, a figure of a couple copulating,
and underneath in hangul: we beget joy, we beget suffering.

It made you want to say a prayer, to conjure prayer.

Lost everything: this is the night; it doesn't love me
or not. Shadow of a hawk, then shadow of a hawk.
Going down at about the speed of a second hand.)

I thought of my mother ending her days in a hotel room,
scarcely able to breathe. "I'm doing fine
except for the asthma." "It's emphysema, Mom."
"We used to call it asthma. Anyway, I'm just lucky
I have my health." Of my brother in the psych ward
at San Francisco General, his ward-mate an eight-month's-pregnant
girl, coming down, like him, from crack.
When they were let out to smoke in a courtyard,
some guy from another ward four stories up
was pounding on the window. She thought he was trying
to get her attention. A shy, pleased smile (gap in her bad front teeth).
And said to me, coyly, "Fatal attraction."
When he got the window open, it turned out
he wanted the orderly, also smoking. He needed insulin.
My brother on crack, spoken with a stutter: "The really crazy jones

lasts about two hours and when you come down,
you really (r-r-r-really) come down. You got nothing left
but the lint in your pockets."

Emptinesses —
one is desire, another is the object that it doesn't have.
Everything real nourished in the space between these things.

There ought to be some single word for the misery of divorce.
(What is the rhythm of that line? Oh, I see. Four and three,
Emily's line! —

>   There ought to be some single word
>   For the misery of divorce.
>   It dines upon you casually
>   duh-dduh-duh-duh-dduh-fierce/remorse/pierce/)

In Berkeley over dinner in a restaurant on a Friday night,
I noticed that it was full of fathers with daughters,
mothers with sons. Some of them people I knew or recognized.
The manager of the bookstore, the woman who sold antiques.
These were the stunned, out-of-the-house, non-cooking parents
in their new apartments who had the children weekends,
while their mates, resuming the unaccustomed ritual of dating,
were out with the new lover. Children, I guess, make of this
what they have to. I looked around. Kids staring at their plates,
parents studying them anxiously, saying, "So, how was school?"

The whole theater of the real: sadness, which seems infinite,
cruelty, which seems infinite, the cheerful one-armed guy
in the bakery mornings—he puts his croissant between his teeth
and pours himself some coffee; someone on the phone
trying to get me to pay my brother's rent, "I got too big a heart,
I try to run a clean place"—the first floor reserved
for transvestite hookers wobbling on spiked heels—
and who would deny their clients the secret exhaustion
of their dreams?; the whole botched world—that funny phrase
I'd heard yesterday, someone talking about a failing baseball team:
'they really screw the pooch.' And the pelicans
that settled in the cove in the late midsummer dusk,
preposterous creatures, they seem companionable,
finding each other as the dark came on. I would go home,
make tea, call my children, some piece of writing
that I'd started would seem possible.

                              Odd how families
live in houses. At first a lot marked out with string.
Then levels, rooms, that lift it off the ground,
arrange it, and then inside that intricate dance
of need and habit and routine. Children's crayon drawings
on the wall. Messages on the refrigerator. Or altars
for the household gods. At night the dreaming bodies,
little gene pool echoes passing back and forth among them,
earlobe, the lap of an eyelid, and the dreams.

Under sorrow, what? I'd think. Under
the animal sense of loss?

                      Climbing in Korea,
months later, coming to the cave of the Sokkaram Buddha —
a view down a forested ravine to the Sea of Japan —
perhaps a glimpse: the closed eyelids — you'd have to make a gesture
with your hand to get the fineness of the gesture in the stone —
the stone hands resting on the thighs, open, utterly composed.

Cool inside. Dark. The stone, though there was no lighting,
seemed to glow. It seemed I could leave every internal fury there
and walk away. In the calm I felt like a wind-up monkey.
Like I had always been a wind-up monkey, and that,
if I knew the gesture (going outside? picking the petals
of the wildflowers — there was something like a thimbleberry bush —
everything was 'like' something I knew — on the path
from the monastery — so I seemed to be walking
in a parallel universe, peopled by unfamiliar bird song,
and ancient trail dust, and the forest's dappled light —
papery flowers, very plain ancestor of the garden rose —
another elaboration of desire — of a startling magenta-blue;
I thought I might pick them, bring them in,
and drop them before the — what — the Buddha —
the carved, massive stone, the —)

Also thought I could leave my wedding ring. And didn't do it.
In the months we were apart, I had endless fantasies

about when I'd finally take it off and how. And then one day,
I was moving, lugging cardboard boxes, I looked down
and it wasn't there. I looked in the grass of the driveway strip.
Sowbugs, an earwig. So strange. This was a time when,
in the universities, everyone was reading Derrida.
Who'd set out to write a dissertation about time;
he read Heidegger, Husserl, Kant, Augustine, and found
that there was no place to stand from which to talk about it.
There was no ground. It was language. The scandal
of nothingness! Put cheerfully to work by my colleagues
to dismantle regnant ideologies. It was a time when,
a few miles away, kids were starting to kill each other
in wars over turf for selling drugs, schizophrenics
with matted hair, dazed eyes, festering feet, always engaged
in some furious volleying inner dialogue they neglected,
unlike the rest of us, to hide, were beginning to fill the streets,
'de-institutionalized,' in someone's idea of reform,
and I was searching in the rosebed of a rented house
inch by inch, looking under the carseat where the paper clips
and Roosevelt dimes and unresolved scum-shapes of once
vegetal stuff accumulate in abject little villages
where matter hides while it transforms itself. Nothing there.
I never found it.

                Looking at old frescoes
from medieval churches in The Cloisters once, I wondered if,
all over Europe, there were not corresponding vacancies,
sheer blanks where pietas and martyrdoms of Santa Lucia
and crowing cocks rising to announce the dawn in which

St. Peter had betrayed his lord in sandstone and basalt
and carnelian marble once had been. This emptiness
felt like that. Under the hosannahs and the terror of the plague
and the crowning of the Virgin in the spring.
I didn't leave my ring. Apparently I was supposed to wait
until it disappeared. I didn't know what else, exactly,
I could leave.
                     In Seoul, in Myongdong, in a teeming alley,
there was a restaurant where the fish was so fresh
they let you know it by beginning each meal
with a small serving of the tips of the tentacles
of octopus, just cut, writhing on a plate.
In the latticed entrance, perch glowing like pearls
in the lamplight thrown from doorways
as they circulated, wide-eyed and moony, in the tanks,
coppery lobsters scuttling over lobsters,
squid like the looseness in a dream. Had been at a meeting
all day on the conditions of imprisoned writers.
This one without paper and pen for several years.
This one with blood in his urine.
                              In small cells
all over the world, I found myself thinking,
walking through the market place—apple-pears
and nectarines in great piles, wavery under swinging lamps,
as if you could sell the sunrise—torturers upholding
the order of the state. Under screams order, and under that—
it must be the torturer's nightmare—nothing.

                                                  Smoothness
of the stone at Sokkaram. The way the contours, flowing,
were weightless and massive at once. I said to myself
there was kindness in the Buddha's hands, but there wasn't kindness
in the hands. They made the idea of kindness
seem — not a delusion exactly, or a joke. They smoothed
the idea away the way you'd stroke a nervous or a frightened dog.

(Outside again. Rubbing my eyes. Deep night, brilliant stars.
I never thought I'd write about this subject. Was tired of
    'subjects.'
Mallarmé on music: the great thing is that it can resolve an
    argument
without ever stating the terms. But thought I'd ride this rhythm
    out,
this somewhat tired, subdued voice — like Landor's "Carlino,"
    perhaps —
a poet-guide! — and see where it was going.)
                                        Around that time —
find the neutral distance in which to say this —
a woman came into my life. What I felt was delight.
When she came into the room, I smiled. The gift was
that there didn't need to be passionate yearning across distances.
One night — before or after Sokkaram? — when we had made love
and made love, desperate kissings, wells of laughter,
in a monkish apartment on the wooden floor, we went outside,
naked in the middle of the night. There must have been a full moon.

                            [55   ]

There was a thick old shadowy deodar cedar by my door
and the cones were glowing, lustrously glowing,
and we thought, both of us, our happiness had lit the tree up.

The word that occurs to me is 'droll.' It seemed sublimely droll.
The way we were as free as children playing hide and seek.
Her talk—raffish, funny, unexpected, sometimes wise, darkened—
the way a black thing is scintillant in light—by irony.
The way neither of us needed to hold back, think
before we spoke, lie, tiptoe carefully around a given subject,
or brace ourselves to say hard truths. It felt to me hilarious,
and hilarity, springwater gushing up from some muse's font
of crystal in old poems, seemed a form of emptiness. Look!
(Rilke in the sonnets) I last but a minute. I walk on nothing.
Coming and going I do this dance in air. At night
when we had got too tired to talk, were touching all along our bodies,
nodding off, I'd fall asleep smiling. Mornings—for how long—
I'd wake in pain. Physical pain, fluid; it moved
through my body like a grassfire spreading on a hill.
(Opposite of touching). I'd think of my wife, her lover,
some moment in our children's lives, the gleam of old wood
on a Welsh cabinet we'd agonized over buying,
put against one wall, then another till it found its place.
This—old word!—riding that we made, its customs, villages,
     demesnes.
would torture me awhile. If she were there, rare mornings
that she was—we did a lot of car keys, hurried dressing, last kisses
on swollen lips at 2 AM—I'd turn to her, stare at her sleeping face

and want to laugh from happiness. I'd even think: ten years
from now we could be screaming at each other in a kitchen,
and want to laugh. My legs and chest still felt as if
someone had been beating them with sticks. I could hardly move.
I'd quote Vallejo to myself: '*Golpes como del odio de Dios*';
I'd stare at the ceiling, bewildered, and feel a grief
so old it could have been some beggar woman in a fairy tale.
I didn't know you could lie down in such swift, opposing currents.

               Also two emptinesses, I suppose, the one
joy comes from, the one regret, disfigured intention, the longing
to be safe or whole flows into when it's disappearing.

I'd gone out of the cave. Looked at the scaled brightness
of the sea ten miles away; looked at unfamiliar plants.
During the war, a botanist in Pusan had told me,
a number of native species had become extinct. People
in the countryside boiled anything that grew to make a soup.
We had 'spring hunger,' he said, like medieval peasants.
There's even a word for it in ancient Korean. Back inside,
in the cool darkness carved with boddhisattvas,
I presented myself once more for some revelation.
Nothing. Great calm, flowing stone. No sorrow, no not-sorrow.
Lotuses, carved in the pediment, simple, fleshy, open.

Private pain is easy, in a way. It doesn't go away,
but you can teach yourself to see its size. Invent a ritual.
Walk up a mountain in the afternoon, gather up pine twigs.

Light a fire, thin smoke, not an ambitious fire,
and sit before it and watch it till it burns to ash
and the last gleam is gone from it, and dark falls.
Then you get up, brush yourself off, and walk back to the world.
If you're lucky, you're hungry.
                                        In the town center
of Kwangju, there was a late October market fair.
Some guy was barbecuing halfs of baby chicks on a long, sooty
        contraption
of a grill, slathering them with soy sauce. Baby chicks.
Corn pancakes stuffed with leeks and garlic. Some milky,
violent, sweet Korean barley wine or beer. Families strolling.
Booths hawking calculators, sox, dolls to ward off evil,
and computer games. Everywhere, of course, it was Korea,
people arguing politics, red-faced, women serving men.
I thought in this flesh-and-charcoal-scented heavy air
of the Buddha in his cave. Tired as if from making love
or writing through the night. Was I going to eat a baby chick?
Two pancakes. A clay mug of the beer. Sat down
under an umbrella and looked to see, among the diners
feasting, quarreling about their riven country,
if you were supposed to eat the bones. You were. I did.

JATUN SACHA

First she was singing. Then it was a gold thing, her singing.
And her bending. She was singing and a gold thing.
A selving. It was a ringing before there was a bell.

Before there was a bell there was a bell. Notwithstanding.
Standing or sitting, sometimes at night or in the day,
when they worked, they hummed. And made their voices high
and made sounds. It was the ringing they hadn't heard yet
singing, though they had heard it, ringing.

When Casamiro's daughter went to the river and picked arum
    leaves,
and wet them, and rubbed them together,
they made the one sweet note that was the ringing.
It was the one-note cry of a bee-eating bird
with a pale blue crest, and when the first one
made the ringing with the arum leaves, and the others
heard that the arum leaves were the bee-eating bird,
they laughed. Their laughter rang.

And the young guy who worked metal—they liked it best at night,
when the iron glowed and the sparks showered down
and he struck metal against metal in the glowing.

He fashioned what he fashioned for adornment
or for praying or for killing. And he knew the made things
from the ringing. Which was the arum leaves and the sounds
made in love and the bee-eating bird and the humming.

She sang like that, something of keening and something of
    laughing,
birth cries, and a gold thing, ringing.

FRIDA KAHLO: IN THE SALIVA

In the saliva
In the paper
in the eclipse
In all the lines
in all the colors
in all the clay jars
in my breast
outside inside —
in the inkwell — in the difficulties of writing
in the wonder of my eyes — in the ultimate
limits of the sun (the sun has no limits) in
everything. To speak it all is imbecile, magnificent
DIEGO in my urine — DIEGO in my mouth — in my
heart. In my madness. in my dream — in
the blotter — in the point of my pen —
in the pencils — in the landscapes — in the
food — in the metal — in imagination
in the sicknesses — in the glass cupboards —
in his lapels — in his eyes — DIEGO —
in his mouth — DIEGO — in his lies.

*Transcribed and translated from a manuscript in her hand, at Diego Rivera's studio near the
Hacienda San Angel in Mexico City*

ENGLISH: AN ODE

1.

　　¿De quien son las piedras del rio
que ven tus ojos, habitante?

Tiene un espejo la mañana.

2.

Jodhpurs: from a state in northeast India,
for the riding breeches of the polo-playing English.

Dhoti: once the dress of the despised,
it is practically a symbol of folk India.
One thinks of blood flowering in Gandhi's
after the zealot shot him.

Were one, therefore, to come across a child's primer
a rainy late winter afternoon in a used bookshop
in Hyde Park and notice, in fine script,
fading, on the title page,
"Susanna Mansergh, The Lodge, Little Shelford, Cmbs."

and underneath it, a fairly recent ball-point
in an adult hand: *Anna Sepulveda Garcia — sua libra*
and flip through pages which asseverate,
in captions enhanced by lively illustrations,
that *Jane wears jodhpurs,* while *Derek wears a dhoti,*
it wouldn't be unreasonable to assume a political implication,

lost, perhaps, on the children of Salvadoran refugees
studying English in a housing project in Chicago.

3.

Ode: not connected, historically, to *odor* or to *odd.*

To *mad,* though obsolete, meant "to behave insanely"
and is quite another thing than to *madden,*
meaning, of course, "to irritate."
So that the melancholy Oxford cleric who wished to live
"Far from the madding crowd's ignoble strife"
and gave Thomas Hardy the title for that novel
was merely observing that people in large numbers
living at close quarters act crazy
and are best given a wide berth.

Not an option, perhaps,
for a former high school math teacher
from San Salvador whose sister, a secretary in the diocesan office

of the Christian Labor Movement, was found
in an alley with her neck broken, and who therefore
followed her elder brother to Chicago and, perhaps,
bought a child's alphabet book in a used bookstore
near the lake where it had languished for thirty years
since the wife, perhaps, of an Irish professor of Commonwealth
   History
at the university had sold it in 1959—maybe the child died
of some childhood cancer—maybe she outgrew the primer
and when her bookshelf began to fill with more grown-up books,
The Wind in the Willows, Winnie-the-Pooh—
what privilege those titles suddenly call up!—
her father, famous for his groundbreaking *Cold War and Commonwealth*
of 1948, looking antique now on the miscellaneous shelf
beside row on row of James T. Farrell, sold it. Or perhaps his wife
did and found it painful to let her daughter's childhood go,
was depressed after. Probably she hated Chicago anyway.
And, browsing, embittered, among the volumes on American history
she somehow felt she should be reading,
thought *Wisconsin, Chicago:* they killed them
and took their language and then they used it
to name the places that they've taken.
Perhaps the marriage survived. Back in London
she may have started graduate school in German Lit.
"Be ahead of all partings," Rilke said in the Spender translation.
Perhaps she was one of those lives—if the child did die
of the sickness I chose to imagine—in which death
inscribes a permanent before and after. Perhaps

she was one of those whose story is innocence
and a private wound and aftermath.

4.

-*Math,* as it turned out,
when she looked up the etymolology
comes from an Anglo-Saxon word for mowing.
Maeth. It would have been the era
of "hot skirts" and The Rolling Stones.
And she a little old to enjoy it. Standing on Chelsea Embankment
after the Duncan Grant retrospective at the Tate,
thinking about the use of *∂u* in the *Duino Elegies*
or about the photo in the *Times* that morning
of the Buddhist monk in Saigon, wearing something
like a dhoti, immobile, sheathed in flames.

5.

There are those who think it's in fairly bad taste
to make habitual reference to social and political problems
in poems. To these people it seems a form of melodrama
or self-aggrandizement, which it no doubt partly is.
And there's no doubt either that these same people also tend
to feel that it ruins a perfectly good party
to be constantly making reference to the poor or oppressed

and their misfortunes in poems which don't,
after all, lift a finger to help them. Please
help yourself to the curried chicken.
What is the etymology of *curry*? Of *chicken*?
Wouldn't you like just another splash of chardonnay?
There's far less objection, generally speaking,
you will find yourself less *at loggerheads*
with the critics, by making mention of accidental death,
which might happen to any of us, which does not,
therefore, seem like moral nagging, and which is also,
in our way of seeing things, possibly tragic
and possibly absurd—"Helen Mansergh was thinking about
   Rilke's pronouns
which may be why she never saw the taxi"—and thus
a subject much easier to ironize.

She—the mother from Salvador—may have bought several books.
Mother Goose, Goodnight, Moon. All
relatively cheap. And that night her brother might have come
with a bag of groceries. And—a gesture against sleet and ice—
flowers in January!
And the Salvadoran paper from Miami.

   6.

Disaster: something wrong with the stars.

Loggerheads: heavy brass balls attached to long sticks;
they were heated on shipboard and plunged into buckets of tar
to soften it for use. By synecdoche were sailors tars.
And from the rage of living together in brutish conditions
on a ship the tars were often at loggerheads. You could crush
a man's knees with them easily. One swing. Claim
it was an accident. If the buggers didn't believe you,
the punishment was some number of lashes with a whip. Not
   death.
That was the punishment for sodomy, or striking an officer.

   7.

                    "As when the Sun
in dim eclipse disastrous twilight sheds . . . "
Mount Diablo foothills, green in the early spring.
Creeks running, scent of bay leaves in the air.

And we heard a high two-note whistle: once,
twice, and then again with a high vibrato tailing.
"What's that?" "Loggerhead shrike."

(Years later one of the young poets at Iowa, impatient
with her ornithologist boyfriend, his naming
everything to death, her thinking *bird, bird!*)

8.

Imagine (from the Latin, *imago*, a likeness)
a language (also from Latin, *lingua*, the tongue)
purged (*purgo*, to cleanse) of history (not the Greek *hist*
for tissue, but the Greek *historia*,
to learn by inquiry). Not this net of circumstance
(*circum*, etc) that we are caught in,
ill-starred, quarried with veins of cruelty,
stupidity, bad luck,
which rhymes with *fuck*,
not the sweet act, the exclamation
of disgust, or maybe both
a little singing ode-like rhyme
because we live our lives in language and in time,
craving some pure idiomorphic dialect of the thing itself,
Adamic, electrified by clear tension
like the distance between a sparrow and a cat,
self and thing and eros as a god of wonder:
it sat upon a branch and sang: the bird.

9.

In one of Hardy's poems, a man named "Drummer Hodge,"
born in Lincolnshire where the country word
for twilight was *dimpsy* two centuries ago,
was a soldier buried in Afghanistan.

Some war that had nothing to do with him.
Face up according to the custom of his people
so that Hardy could imagine him gazing forever
into foreign constellations. *Cyn* was the Danish word
for farm. Hence Hodge's cyn.
And someone of that stock studied medicine.
Hence Hodgkin's lymphoma. *Lymph* from the Latin
meant once "a pure clear spring of water."
Hence *limpid*. But it came to mean
the white cells of the blood.

>"His homely Northern breast and brain
>Grow to some Southern tree
>And strange-eyed constellations reign
>His stars eternally."

10.

I have been hearing it all morning
As if it were a Spanish nonsense rhyme.
Like the poem of José Martí the woman in Chicago
might have sung to her children as they fell asleep:

>Yo soy un hombre sincero
>De donde crece la palma,
>Y antes de morime quiero
>Echar mis versos del alma.

Do you hear it? She has (strong beat)
a Hodg (strong beat) kin's lym-phom (strong beat)-a.

This impure spring of language, strange-eyed,
"To scatter the verses of the soul."

   11.

So—what are the river stones
that come swimming to your eyes, *habitante*?

They hold the hope of morning.

THE SEVENTH NIGHT

It was the seventh night and he walked out to look at stars.
Chill in the air, sharp, not of summer, and he wondered
if the geese on the lake felt it and grew restless
and if that was why, in the late afternoon, they had gathered
at the bay's mouth and flown abruptly back and forth,
back and forth on the easy, swift veering of their wings.
It was high summer and he was thinking of autumn,
under a shadowy tall pine, and of geese overhead on cold mornings
and high clouds drifting. He regarded the stars in the cold dark.
They were a long way off, and he decided, watching them blink,
that compared to the distance between him and them,
the outside-looking-in feeling was dancing cheek-to-cheek.
And noticed then that she was there, a shadow between parked
   cars,
looking out across the valley where the half-moon poured thin light
down the pine ridge. She started when he approached her,
and then recognized him, and smiled, and said, "Hi, night light."
And he said, "Hi, dreamer." And she said, "Hi, moonshine,"
and he said, "Hi, mortal splendor." And she said, "That's good."
She thought for a while. Scent of sage or yerba buena
and the singing in the house. She took a new tack and said,
"My father is a sad chair and I am the blind thumb's yearning."
He said, "Who threw the jade swan in the boiling oatmeal?"

Some of the others were coming out of the house, saying goodbye,
hugging each other. She said, "The lion of grief paws
what meat she is given." Cars starting up, one of the stagehands
struggling to uproot the pine. He said, "Rifling the purse
of possible regrets." She said, "Staggering tarts, a narcoleptic
    moon."
Most of the others were gone. A few gathered to listen.
The stagehands were lugging off the understory plants.
Two others were rolling up the mountain. It was clear that,
though polite, they were impatient. He said, "Goodbye, last thing."
She said, "So long, apocalypse." Someone else said, "Time,"
but she said, "The last boat left Xania in late afternoon."
He said, "Goodbye, Moscow, nights like sable,
mornings like the word *persimmon*." She said,
"Day's mailman drinks from a black well of reheated coffee
in a cafe called Mom's on the outskirts of Durango." He said,
"That's good." And one of the stagehands stubbed
his cigarette and said, "OK, would the last of you folks to leave,
if you can remember it, just put out the stars?" which they did,
and the white light everywhere in that silence was white paper.

INTERRUPTED MEDITATION

Little green involute fronds of fern at creekside.
And the sinewy clear water rushing over creekstone
of the palest amber, veined with a darker gold,
thinnest lines of gold rivering through the amber
like—ah, now we come to it. *We were not put on earth,*
the old man said, he was hacking into the crust
of a sourdough half loaf in his vehement, impatient way
with an old horn-handled knife, *to express ourselves.*
I knew he had seen whole cities leveled: also
that there had been a time of shame for him, outskirts
of a ruined town, half Baroque, half Greek Revival,
pediments of Flora and Hygeia from a brief eighteenth-century
health spa boom lying on the streets in broken chunks
and dogs scavenging among them. His one act of courage
then had been to drop pieces of bread or chocolate,
as others did, where a fugitive family of Jews
was rumored to be hiding. *I never raised my voice,*
of course, none of us did. He sliced wedges of cheese
after the bread, spooned out dollops of sour jam
from some Hungarian plum, purple and faintly gingered.
Every day the bits of half-mildewed, dry, hard—
this is my invention—whitened chocolate, dropped furtively

into rubble by the abandoned outbuilding of some suburban
mechanic's shop—but I am sure he said chocolate—
and it comforted no one. *We talked in whispers.*
"Someone is taking them." "Yes," Janos said,
"But it might just be the dogs." He set the table.
Shrugged. Janos was a friend from the university,
who fled east to join a people's liberation army,
died in Siberia somewhere. *Some of us whispered 'art',*
he said. *Some of us 'truth.' A debate with cut vocal chords.*
You have to understand that, for all we knew, the Germans
would be there forever. And if not the Germans, the Russians.
Well, you don't 'have to' understand anything, naturally.
No one knew which way to jump. What we had was language,
you see. Some said art, some said truth. Truth, of course,
was death. Clattered the plates down on the table. *No one,*
no one said 'self-expression.' Well, you had your own forms
of indulgence. Didn't people in the forties say 'man'
instead of 'the self?' I think I said. *I thought 'the self'*
came in in 1949. He laughed. *It's true. Man,*
we said, is the creature who is able to watch himself
eat his own shit from fear. You know what that is?
Melodrama. I tell you, there is no bottom to self-pity.

This comes back to me on the mountainside. Butterflies—
tiny blues with their two-dot wings like quotation marks
or an abandoned pencil sketch of a face. They hover lightly
over lupine blooms, whirr of insects in the three o'clock sun.
What about being? I had asked him. *Isn't language responsible*

to it, all of it, the texture of bread, the hairstyles
of the girls you knew in high school, shoelaces, sunsets,
the smell of tea? Ah, he said, you've been talking to Milosz.
To Czeslaw I say this: silence precedes us. We are catching up.
I think he was quoting Jabes whom he liked to read.
Of course, here, gesturing out the window, pines, ragged green
of a winter lawn, the bay, you can express what you like,
enumerate the vegetation. And you! you have to, I'm afraid,
since you don't excel at metaphor. A shrewd, quick glance
to see how I have taken this thrust. You write well, clearly.
You are an intelligent man. But —finger in the air —
silence is waiting. Milosz believes there is a Word
at the end that explains. There is silence at the end,
and it doesn't explain, it doesn't even ask. He spread chutney
on his bread, meticulously, out to the corners. Something
angry always in his unexpected fits of thoroughness
I liked. Then cheese. Then a lunging, wolfish bite.
Put it this way, I give you, here, now, a magic key.
What does it open? This key I give you, what exactly
does it open? Anything, anything! But what? I found
that what I thought about was the failure of my marriage,
the three or four lost years just at the end and after.
For me there is no key, not even the sum total of our acts.
But you are a poet. You pretend to make poems. And?

She sat on the couch sobbing, her rib cage shaking
from its accumulated abysses of grief and thick sorrow.
I don't love you, she said. The terrible thing is

that I don't think I ever loved you. He thought to himself
fast, to numb it, that she didn't mean it, thought
what he had done to provoke it. It was May.
Also pines, lawn, the bay, a blossoming apricot.
Everyone their own devastation. Each on its own scale.
I don't know what the key opens. I know we die,
and don't know what is at the end. We don't behave well.
And there are monsters out there, and millions of others
to carry out their orders. We live half our lives
in fantasy, and words. This morning I am pretending
to be walking down the mountain in the heat.
A vault of blue sky, traildust, the sweet medicinal
scent of mountain grasses, and at trailside —
I'm a little ashamed that I want to end this poem
singing, but I want to end this poem singing — the wooly
closed-down buds of the sunflower to which, in English,
someone gave the name, sometime, of pearly everlasting.

NOTES

Dragonflies Mating. Jaime de Angulo was a well-known folklorist and collector of native California myths and stories. I owe this story about him to my friend Malcolm Margolin.

Regalia for a Black Hat Dancer. The shrine of the Buddha of Sokkaram is situated on a mountaintop near Kyongju, forty miles inland from Pusan and the site of one of Korea's oldest Buddhist monasteries.

Jatun Sacha. The title comes from the name of a biological study center in the Ecuadorian rainforest on the Rio Napo near the town of Tena.

English: An Ode. The lines in Spanish come from a poem by the Mexican poet Pura López Colomé in her book *Un Cristal en Otro,* Ediciones Toledo, Mexico City, 1989.

The Seventh Night. I borrowed the phrase "staggering tarts" from Mary Karr, with her permission.

ABOUT THE AUTHOR

ROBERT HASS is the author of three books of poems, *Field Guide* (1973), *Praise* (1979), and *Human Wishes* (1989). He has co-translated several volumes of poetry by Czeslaw Milosz, including *Unattainable Earth* and *Provinces*, and contributed to *Dante's Inferno: Translations by Twenty Contemporary Poets*. He has edited *Selected Poems: 1954–1986* by Tomas Tranströmer, as well as *The Essential Haiku: Versions of Basho, Buson, and Issa*. A book of his essays, *Twentieth Century Pleasures*, received the National Book Critics Circle Award for Criticism in 1984. His many honors include a John D. and Catherine T. MacArthur Fellowship. In 1995 he was selected by the Library of Congress as Poet Laureate of the United States. Robert Hass teaches at the University of California at Berkeley.